Welcoming Oneness

When thy di-vine selves walk hand in hand
Living The Father's First Command
The Mother's Veils shall slip away
Welcoming Oneness to a New Day

Welcoming Oneness

Carena del Uno

To order additional copies of this book, contact:
Xlibris Corporation
1-888-795-4274
www.Xlibris.com
Orders@Xlibris.com
128049

Contents

Prologue

From Where Came This?

Because I was the doer
I thought the writing was mine
But wherefrom came the creative thought
That entered it into my mind?

We are so used to limiting our thinking
To the material world we see
That we cease to wonder how or where
Our ideas came to be.

Did they flash through space from another world
Through a mind in a far galaxy
Or did they spiral down from a higher plane
To my inner self and me?

And which of my myriad feelings
Can I truly say are mine
As some might come from challenged folks
While others from angels divine?

For if we believe that God is One
Without division or end
Wherein does our separateness lie
This Truth of Being to rend?

And then, if we really thought
This concept of Oneness through
We might begin to wonder where
The limits are of the real me or you.

So be an expression
Of the One Consciousness that IS
And in love and humility
Glorify the Wholeness that is His.

Dedication:

To the many people who have helped me understand a bit more of life

and all the love I've been blessed with in the process—from here on

the earth plane, and from my loved ones who are topside. Thank you.

Chapter 1

Perspectives

When Integrity within The Good
is thine uppermost Key
Then all your perceptions
will bring you closer to Me

Echoes Of Perspectives

Who of you do I see
An outer perspective of me?
Or do I view
But an echo of you—
A ring of your past
Becoming at last—

    A new present . . . .

And if I'm within my core or centered Self
Can I witness something on a hidden shelf
And coax it out of its self imagined perdition
Into a state of freedom for wisdom's fruition?

Mind And Heart

Mind Speaks:

I see the world through the rods in my eyes
Creating patterns that may or may not be wise
They out-picture themselves in black and white
In symbols and forms as I work toward the Light

With discipline I gain a power both far-sighted and rare
As I look into the future toward more rarified air
But the creations I make stay within my time and space
Fostering a duality not always to my taste

With a magician's rod, I am ego, the ruler of my created world
I can build for myself or humanity when my power's unfurled

Heart Speaks:

Colored by the cones in my eyes
I see beauty without guise
Within a loving field
Surrounding a God unsealed

I live to know my heart of love
And stay in communion with the heavenly dove
So that Higher can direct the whole of me
And exchange my self's fate for soul's destiny

I am a part of a wondrous whole
And Divine Brotherhood is ever my goal

At The Back Of Every Door . . .

At the back of every door of tests and trials
          are blessings and benedictions

At the back of every door of ignorance
          is consciousness awakening

At the back of every door of fear and trepidation
          are the release of burdens and expanding wisdom

At the back of every door of imagined loss
          is Love's imperishable totality

At the back of every door of dependence
          is Self Realization and Responsibility

At the back of every door of material existence
          is a life of purposeful Good

At the back of every door of mind's emptiness
          is the Essence of The Unknown GOD

At the back of every door of transition or death
          is Greater Life Becoming

The Cycle Of Life

The newborn sees where his nourishment is
A child sees the world as his

A teen wants all his self-conceived rights
A young adult wants a partner to give him delights

In time maturity approaches his self-centered play
And he sees others' sovereignty enter its array

So when senior-hood finally peeks around the bend
His wisdom and compassion have begun to ascend

Wherein he loves others in self-made worlds as was his
And give them their freedom to learn from that which Is

Then with heart attuned and mind focused on the grail
With Godlike senses he glides through illusion's veil

To become part of the endless love that the newborn knows
And the eternal singleness from which eternity flows

Within The Love Of Self

Within the Heart of Being
There reigns a way of seeing
Where loss is unknown
And lack is outgrown
Where competition is a forgotten outer dream
And the love of God relaxes each scene
Where comparison and judgment of outer fields
Pass by the wayside as conscious oneness congeals

You might ask with your human mind
Can any of this be accomplished in time?

Life's just a mind set, would be my reply
A choice in God's Love that enables one to fly
To see the inner being of each and all you meet
And embrace them as free spirits within heaven's seat

Do this and your world will make a godly shift
As you cross a subjectively veiled rift
Where the human replaces his self-enhancing race
With Unity and Love and the Mother's Compassionate Grace

Riches

What need have I for gold in my hands
When the consciousness of the Sun warms our lands

And which silver gives me the most delight
The coins in my pocket or the stars at night

The green of printed paper as it mounts up in banks
Or the new green of springtime for which all nature gives thanks

True wealth is in consciousness and cannot be measured
By material things to which our outer mind is tethered

For money is just mans bridge in time and space
Whose importance evaporates when we live in God's Grace

And do those things to which our souls most aspire
With heart and mind married in harmonious desire

Oh what a joy-filled world it will be
When we all live in Oneness and are sovereignly Free

Is this but a dream? Can its goal ever be actualized?
Indubitably my friend, or it couldn't have been conceptualized!

Hide And Seek

Hide and Seek
Open and Find
Conceal or Reveal
The Fruit or the Peel

Towards The Core

The closer you are to the core of Oneness
The Truer the Love you will access
And even if your focus is but singly united
The whole of consciousness will be blessed

Big Fish—Little Fish

When I think I'm a big fish in my little pond
May I retrieve the humility to go one step beyond
So that once more I can truly be Me
A little golden fish in a Great Cosmic Sea

Open Your Mind

Open your mind
So that you can float
On the breath of God
And become The Word of God

Replacing Judgment With Divine Conception

I don't "no"
Because I can't know
That which is true and real
And that which is an impression congealed

Until I do
Influenced by my humanness
Much of my perception
is based on my own limitation

Thus I try to hold an image
Of the divine conception
Of a person or situation
So that it will be in harmonious relation
To the Infinite Good

Blessings

Blessings are ever there
        Constant and all pervading

Evaporate your self into them
        And sweet harmony you'll be aiding

Preparing For Heaven

Act down here as if you were in heaven
Where all is for Good and God is your leaven
Where thoughts are noble and grace prevails
And beauty can be seen through self-imposed veils

For truly if God is One and Consciousness is Whole
How can heaven be separate from the universe we know
God's Goodness as fact must be everywhere underlying
So stop giving credence to the illusions you're buying

They entered your mind when ego came into play
And self and its protection joined free will's display
'Tis time to release all separateness and temporal power
And accept God's Divine Oneness as your rightful dower

So as each new year awakens and its seeds sprout into spring
May we prepare ourselves for heaven and the ideals it brings
Taking responsibility for a positive love-filled mending
Rather than waiting on another for a fairytale ending

Thus can we co-create a heaven on our beloved earth
As we make a resolution to work toward our divine rebirth

The Laughing Buddha

You think the laughing Buddha isn't wise
And his full belly is just a disguise
No, my friend, for in his truth he knows
That his world is made up of self taught shows
Wherein he can partake of all that is
Enlightening it with humor and making it his

For God excludes nothing and no one from His sight
But smiles at his children in their willful birthright
Encompassing them in unconditional love
In the knowledge that one day they'll rise above
Their lesser self's whirled wind of imagined show
And follow His Laws patterning them to grow

So be as this Buddha, who sits at heaven's gate
And laugh at the scenes your comrades create
Knowing that one day all of their self imagined fate
Will become the Destiny the Laughing Buddha ate

Chapter 2

Beauty

The Rose Bush

Though the physical bush may look prickly and old

And was pruned by nature along life's way

Its heart still sings softly of beauty untold

Unfurling its soul love and blessing the day

Love Is A Blossom

Love is a forever blossom on the Tree of Life
        sitting so gently and lightly on its perch
                that the Tree hardly is aware that it's there.

White, tender, soft—with a fragrance so sweet
        that senses less than pure would know not its essence.

Ever Beautiful

Gave the aspen freely
      their leaves to sun and earth
To stand at water's edge so truly
      though naked on their berth

But then though eyes of heartfelt love
      I looked at them again
And saw them in their golden gowns
      freed of season's wend

More alive and beautiful were they now
      within our field of love
Within a dream, an altared scene
      enfolding us from above

Then from on High or deep within
      two words caressed my being
And with feeling both tender and true
      sweet tears glazed o'er my seeing

"Ever Beautiful—Ever Beautiful"
      rang through Heart's open space
"That's how We see you always:
      Ever Beautiful,
           Within Our Love's Embrace."

Then Love's Baptism took the gentle hand of Peace
and the lake, sun filled and windless, was once again
simply its own paradise on earth . . . .

A Tree's Love

When you walk in a forest between earth and sky
And feel the peace born of seasons gone bye
Of trees standing silent, united in their core
Accepting God's offering of life and its store
It's time to be still, to join with these trees
To let go of your mind-set, relax, be at ease
To attune to truths deeper than your spinning mind
Loosen your human-hood and your clockwork time
Then gentle yourself into heart's true space
Beyond all conquest and self's mundane race

Have you ever thought about a tree getting mad
At a cold autumn wind—and then feeling bad
Absurd, you say, they don't have emotions such as these
Ah, maybe they're wiser, having evolved through dis-ease
Maybe they know that all is for growth and for good
And trust in patience until each experience is understood
For even while the wind is blowing their dead leaves down
Their vast roots are strengthening deep underground

To allow and join the flow and the tide
With heart ever ready and mind opened wide
With trust like the trees, attuned to their core
Yields one a truer life and allows an open door
To understanding the deeper, fuller nature of things
And prepares one to don love's gossamer wings

So take a tip from our brethren the trees
Resist not Love and you'll find but ease
For if God is all and He's only Love
That one attunement will bring you His Dove
Whereby you can fly into subconscious spaces
And work through Heart's angelic embraces
Changing your world in silence and in peace
Through a reverence eternal, that never will cease

Mother Earth

How sensitive is Mother Earth?

> She's as sensitive as the tiny white flowers
> that sprinkle themselves o'er the forest floors
> and as delicate as the gentle blossoms of the
> young peach tree welcoming in the springtime.

> She carries the spectrum of Love.

How protective is Mother Earth?

> She's as protective of life as the mighty oak
> that gives shade from the summer's heat
> and food and shelter to the small creatures
> of the land and sky throughout winter's chill.

> She carries the spectrum of Compassion.

She's as mighty as towering mountains and great granite cliffs.
yet as noble and true as the great redwood trees that form her
magnificent cathedrals.

> She carries the spectrum of Reverence.

She's a venerable living Soul who gives us all a platform for our feet,
nourishment for our bodies, and beauty for our spirit.

Love Her—Honor Her—Respect Her as the True Mother She Is.

Cradle all life in a mother's gentleness
and inharmony will dissolve in love's kindness.

In The Womb Of Space

When at twilight one gazes through the depths of space
And wanders o'er galaxies to distant to embrace

One throbs in heart with wisdom's chill
When, through ones being, very still

Echoes the cadence of worlds yet to be born
In a firmament where sweet awareness is adorned

The New Day

One if by land, Three if by sea
Five for the Fire that sets you free . . . .

Ages of Splendor, not forsaken
By rites and rituals solemnly taken

Pass through the Portal of sages and kings
Where Virtue, Truth, and Harmony take wing

Evolving magnificence in timeless array
The fields of Springtime welcoming The New Day

Daath

A Rose of White adorns you now
With God's Truth telling you when and how

To pass through the Needle both silent and true
Into the realm of thy Essence and the Real You

For timing is ever the earthly Key
When conduct is patterned by Omneity

Yea, the Rose is real on its etheric tree
Expanding the Template for many to see

Yet to eyes still earthly, it remains Unknown
Having given up Its Identity to the Sacred Throne

For in pristine sacred purity, with no color or form
It hands down the Seed from which a Christ is born

Experiencing The Ultimate Joy

Tiny golden flames dancing on the leaves
Ethereal playful undines riding midnight seas
Meadow grasses swaying within a gentle wind
The Mother's loving nature nurturing her kin

Alive is this joy to the uncontrolling
At One in our depths, its Song extolling
Dancing freely in heaven's hallowed domain
Singing life's fullness with each open refrain

Come dance with me now, it echoes from within
Relinquish your self and live free of sin
Love's Sacred Song of Freedom gladly awaits you
In Spirit's realm of creation to joyously embrace you

There you'll be one and in tune with all
The flames of life before mind's fall
Singing with etheric frequencies
Within Love's vital expectancies

Where giving is receiving, before the birth of time
And all are part of God's free flowing Trine
That foreruns the creation surrounding you and me
As the life force inherent in the Great Cosmic Sea

Be one with us now, as ever You Be
Come dance within to Live knowingly
Give thy desires up to the Sun/Son
And allow your whole being to become as One

For underneath all that you see
Is Life's perpetual dancing Tree
Twirling in Love's Grace and Joy's Purity
To Honor The Great One within you and me

Chapter 3

Knowing Me

My Path

Often it's the path on which I travel
That helps to tell me who I am
Yet it's who **I** Am
That leads me unto the path on which I travel.

Man Know Thy Self

Man know thy Self and to that Self be true
Consider it throughout your life as the very best part of you

It's your personal gate to the wholeness of your being
Your guide and escort through life's holographic dreaming

Cushioned by etheric air that flows through fields of time
You sweep through life's lessons of your own self-made wine

And all the while your Self patiently waits
For you to realize the folly of your creates

Then in the service that it divinely pledged to you
It offers will and wisdom to walk to what is true

Sharing your challenges then making them clear
With loving energies to curb indecision and fear

When will it be time to think of this Companion first
Before you gallop out in lust to fill your sensual thirst
When will you share your decisions with it consciously
That your combined energy may be used purposefully

Consider it an honor that God gave you this Self
To journey with you, offering you riches beyond wealth

So man know thy Self and to that Self be true
For in this way, heaven will shine from the soul of you

The Eye I Am

I sit in the center of a circle round
Where light and shadow doth abound

For around me dances my every self
Intermingling on a timeless shelf

All of me interdependent on my one great whole
That many on earth would define as soul

Without my shadows what would I see
But the white light of my own divinity

Uniting together toward the Eye that I Am
Within the All Knowingness of my God to blend

Consecration

The patterns cycling round in the world I see
Are in fact mirrors of the manifest me

The World in Truth that was ordained to be
Becomes Its Self when I'm united with Thee

This happens when the purified chalice
Removes self will and every hint of malice—

Toward any creation animated or still
Allowing its awakening within God-given free will

When Will I Be Clean Enough

When will I be clean enough
To let go of my personal stuff
Not just to let go of outer things
But let go fully so my soul sings

Most of my days are spent in my mind
To do this, to do that, and always be kind
But what would happen if my heart held sway
Would love magnify only good's array
Or would something within me come out to be shown
An act, a judgment, or my shadows full blown

Do I have enough trust to set my self free
Or must I stay burdened by my control of me
Can I walk with courage within my unknown
To open to life's lessons and thus be atoned

This process is inevitable and <u>event</u>ually must be
Before joining with God in the Land of The Free
Where consciously one with the Truth of His Being
I share unwavering Love to creatures still sea-ing

Becoming Who You Are

It's the reach
    That can teach
The process not the goal
    That helps you to unfold

Let it be understood
    That every effort toward the good
Is never lost
    But is embossed
On the fabric of your being
    And the expression you will be seeing

For what is your true goal
    In an eternity that's unending
But the realization of your true Self
    Within your Godhead blending

So be thankful for each challenge
    That appears along your way
For it is but a touchstone
    To create a finer you within a finer day

To The Lord Of The Wind

How wondrous thy path, O master child
That takes you to your goal
How joyous the heart that knows such expanse
Ready for you to unfold

Thy heart in beating—thy mind entreating—
The glories of natures' rare—
A calling supreme, and a change of scene
At-one-ment with the Lord of the Air

Come with me now. Release thy bonds
Step into thy beingness true
With God as your conductor—in perfect harmony
Walk inward to the world that be You

Remove The Trappings

I once looked inside of me
With but desires and form and objects to see
Trapped within the world of self's glee
Where Love and causation were a mystery

As if sealed within a pyramid of old
I was the servant of some lost king
Who commanded my allegiance even after his death
Until my transition would give me wing

This thought-form out-pictured in a recent dream
Wherein my tomb's doors were sealed with stone
Lent fear from entrapment to shroud my mind
Until I felt helpless and alone

But then from within some innermost depth
Came a strength that afore was unknown
The Great Mother of Earth appeared in my thoughts
Who Herself was embedded in form

Yet radiating through pores of space and time
She bloomed through creation her Joy and Grace
Endowing it with Life and a core Divine
Befitting The Father's Embrace

Now philosophers and mystics from ages of yore
Have understood this secret of creation's polarity
That behind the veil of what appears to be
Is its opposite in Light, Love, and Purity

So though The Mother seems blind within all matter
Her consciousness is Awake, Whole and Free
Within the Beauty of her Fulfilled Being
As in Truth yours Is and ever will be

So if thought-forms assail you
Crippling your mind with fear
Remember your Mother within
Lending no illusion your ear

An Unconditional God

God is Unconditional, Self Fulfilling, All One
  Seeing the spectrum of all within
Giving of Himself, His Breath, and His Beingness
  Knowing that all are irrevocably Him.

How can we imitate a GOD such as this
  Within such an infinite frame
Living as we do in a finite world
  And using a limited brain?

Through Unconditional Love comes the Fullness we seek
  Within the Freedom of Being
Where the very essence of Its Wholeness
  Embraces our world of seeing.

But awareness of particulars we've diligently learned
  Through incarnations borne in time
So it's no easy challenge to free false judgments
  From our human analytical mind—

To trust our heart and allow matters to flow
  In their destined, God-guided course
Setting aside self for evolvement's sake
  Without conditions or remorse.

For a Template was seeded within our soul
  Ordaining us to function such as He:
Expansively, Fruitfully, Wisely, Lovingly
  As was His/Our Conception to Be.

So on through lifetimes we persevere
  As particles in an infinite field
Until that day when our Macrocosmic Self
  Will consciously be revealed.

Becoming The I Of Me

How can I manifest my divine potentials
And open to Life's wondrous essentials?

By loving GOD foremost with the whole of you
And exemplifying qualities that are good and true

Then being patient as your old reflections twirl
Around and about your sensory world

All the while do whatever you must
To honor the Laws that you inwardly trust

Fragments of your soul's integrity
Seeding Light, Love, Hope and Charity

God Realization

When you can imitate GOD at His Command
You'll be an awakened Self-realized Man

Otherwise you'll live in a world of hues
Of colored pictures that ensues
From the custom bi-focals that you are wearing
Tainting the environment that you are sharing
Within your self-made world under your migraine sky
Whose exacerbated effects keep your focus from the High

So now you know why mans preface is hued
And can do something about not getting wooed
By external creations of no lasting import
Instead of summoning Wisdom for your escort

So as you journey through this labyrinth of time
Exchange Higher Truths for sodden wine
And carry the Impeccable Flame of Thy Creator
Who is in all ways Mans Wondrous Educator

Transformation

A little worm is full of life as he burrows through verdant green
A minister of humility, he crawls the earth, alone and seldom seen

But all the time in this phase of growth
        he's learning from the depths of the ground
Simple lessons about the life within
        unknown to all who are surfacely gowned

Until finally filled with new understandings rare
He sleeps with dreams of the freedom of air

And imagining beauties he's not seen before
He opens a hidden transformational door

There to awaken in a body that's light and free
Reflecting his inner nature for the world to see

Then with a flap of his wings and a tilt of his head
He arises in beauty his heart's dreams to wed

And once again, with his true self set free
He's demonstrated a wonder of what life can be

Butterflies

We all have the power to spiritually fly
Far beyond our physical sky
So remember when challenges greet your day
That within you are butterflies in beauteous array
That can help you transform the fleeting and untrue
And thereby become more magnificently You.

Chapter 4

The Fall & The Ascension

The Tower

O Thou Bolt of Lightning, magnificent in thy brilliant power,
How simply hast thou drained my ego's cup.

In one fleeting moment did you achieve what years of struggle left wanting,
Crashing my isolated tower and removing my weighty crown.

How captive our illusions are in the framework of our mighty selves
Who live as if they see all that is and are in total control of their destinies—

And though they know they are using but 10% of their brains,
They never question the absolute power of their wills and proficiencies.

The Joining

Where heart will come to me as one
When her love includes all and excludes none

Mind must come two by two
Divinely entwined through and through

Echoing love's life-giving traits
As it greets, then enters, the heavenly gates

Be Mine, Valentine

Be Free
Said my Love to me
Though you will always be mine
It's time to relinquish your wine

Putting your human self
On the shelf
And releasing all fear
For that which is dear

When I gave you a particle of Me
And fashioned within you a Living Tree
I never meant that you should stray
Within creative form and lose your way

But it was a good teaching indeed
So I let you proceed
But now you must begin to turn around
And release the illusions you caused to abound

For My Way is simple, true, and free
Opening to Love for the all of Me
For from that Love were you given life
In pristine form free from strife

A glorious flow
For all to know
Pure consciousness in which to see
What in Totality WE truly be

So give thy heart to the upliftment of the greater
Releasing self to Self in the Now not the later
And become the god you were meant to be
When the whole of you comes back to Me

Beyond The Tools

I don't want to scare you
As that would impair you
For fear is a blind side
That you must deride

But all you can see on the outside
You created on the inside
For you can only see
That of which you be

Yes, GOD <u>did</u> make you perfectly
But in His Love, He set you free
To create a world such as His
With Love and Beauty in all that Is

And so that you'd not remain fools
He gave you inexorable tools
      A mind that's rare
      A creative square
      An emotive force
      And a definite course
      With an inborn passion
      For a world to fashion

The only Law that He demanded
Was that His Love not be remanded
And remain uppermost within you
So these tools remain balanced & true

But forgetting GOD's Selfless Dower
You became absorbed in creative power
And, thinking it was your own
Consciously left his Love, your rightful Home
      To become a di-vine man
      Reaching to infinity and down to sand

Then working with the tools in your charge
You further forgot the central Love at large
Which ever is the one Supernal Key
To return you to Integral Simplicity

So what does this mean in your world today?
Everything that you see that causes you dismay
Is a reflection of your past attitudes, will, & desires
Self-created images which you improperly fired

Thus can your brothers be your fathers
And your sisters be your mothers
Manifesting who you once were
When your memory was a blur

But as members of the same human race
You are all still within GOD's Loving Grace
Separated only by a fraction of time
From the Eternal and the Sublime

To awaken when your undergrowth is transmuted
Rather than judged, ignored, or refuted
And you world is accepted with nobility
As your enlightened responsibility

Then when *yourselves* and *yourself* truly become one
You'll know that the gift of your journey has been won
Therewith to return within True Love's embrace
Until comes your Moment to open a new case

My Reformation

For many years I walked the line
Between self serving and the sublime

My life was mental, my outer mind sharp
I thought I was good but knew not my heart

I soon took a bounce within my manifest world
That humbled me so that my soul could unfurl

Then from out of the clouds above a much feared earth
With the help of the angels, I was given a new birth

I plummeted down to earth's slow and simple seeming
Into the grass roots of Man and The Mother's Love-filled Being

At first I missed the visions and light energy from on high
But like the Indians of old found my purpose by and by

Not to be aloof and manipulate life by a mental string
But to care for all within it that with harmony they might sing

At last I was permitted to open a long sought loving gate
And co-create with God, freed from lives of karmic fate

To keep lower thoughts and emotions out of harm's way
So my soul's conscious efforts would not again go astray

This is what we all want and with angelic help from Higher
We offer up our free will now to manifest our souls' desire

That our ordained time on the physical plane be not in vain
And that only goodness and beauty shall eternally reign

Mind—Cause Or Effect?

Of which is Mind, Root Cause or Effect?
And did Inspiration with "Time" initially connect?
Cometh first the Seed, a Conception of the Divine,
All events and cycles to later de-fine??

Or could Creation have been a way less known
With the Culmination certain and fully blown?
If this be the case, then Mind's progressive chase
Would be due to a cause beneath its self scrutinized face.

So as life's droplet in the mystic's pool reflects its circles round
Think clearly upon the Spool and the coherent ground
From which you now are considering to depart
When each point with the other is an integral part.

For only when perfectly centered with all as your own
With Love and Understanding will you truly be Home
As Duality's Pillars, the Sentinels of Perfection's Scheme
Are united in the Oneness of God's Pristine Dream

The Grand Ascension

Mind Speaks:

> Like the light of a star
> Shining from afar
> The Higher Plane calls to me
> Distant though it may be
> I will refine and set myself free . . . .

> *I will ascend!*

Heart Speaks:

> With the loving acceptance of a Mother for her own
> I open myself to all in God's earthly home
> Then one with Love Supreme
> We become an infallible team
> Fulfilling an Eternal Dream . . . .

> *As we ascent together.*

The Impersonal Door

When resonant frequencies in the fullness of Heart's space
Do a dance within the Mother's Loving Embrace
The Father becomes in-filled with unfathomable delight
And breathes unto Life the Breath of Pristine Light

Then for us, measurement becomes no more
And the personal enters the impersonal door
And all of our former separate seeing
Becomes fused in One Divine Sentient Being

When Spirit Sings

When Spirit sings
And Thought takes wings
Will becomes true
And Love is renewed
For raised to the Sun
Her Creative Process has begun

A Word and a Divine Refrain
Then echoes through Heaven's Domain
Where, gathering heartfelt emotion
It becomes a drop of Celestial Ocean
Condensing within each responding heart
The seed of a resplendent co-creative art

There it must silently reside
Awaiting dispersion in the world outside
In that hour when Altruism weds the Light
Furnishing Goodness its Divine Birthright

And as this drop of sunlit dew
Amalgamates and blesses the earth anew
It also lightens the Sacred Chalice
That went through the seeming retort
In order to bring it forth

Consummated

All the stars in the night sky shining
Merge within Me
To become the Light of my Central Sun
As the God of my Being
Breathes in His Great Breath of Life

All the feelings and faces in my world exposed
Unite as One
To become the Great Central Sea within Me
In Rapture with the Heartbeat of Life

I am Homeward bound.

Chapter 5

Emotions, Will, & Desire

Emotions

Joy, Love, Peace, and Trust are the universal norm
All other emotions are polarized and humanly born

Certainly duality exists in the higher spheres
For manifestation to creation is very dear
And the matrix of self and its curiosity
Can promote understanding and sagacity
The trick is to be able to step out of their propensities
Before becoming scattered within their polar densities

So how is this done?
By knowing that all are one
And centering inside The Core of all
There to respond to Its Omniscient Call
For the manifest play
Is meant to be <u>God's</u> display

So instead of just drifting
Practice shifting
From the objective outside to the Oneness within
To formulate responses apart from human din
And in thoughts and feelings practice purposeful sifting
Letting go of thought-forms that aren't truly uplifting

Remember that whoever you see
Is ultimately one with the I of thee
And should be met with Heart's true emotions
From the Mother's Universal Oceans
Of Joy, Love, Peace and Trust
The Golden Elixirs of Angelic Dust

Desires

Food is a magnetic plate
That opens the foundational gate
                To desires false or true
Nourishing mind toward its centered core
Or fueling the senses to want ever more
                While hiding the real you

Balance is the silver key to a knowing sensitivity
Where will and desire can meet in gentle serenity

Then thy crosses of branches four
Become symmetrical around their living core
And its central sacred flame
Can envelope the fullness of Thy True Name

So test their good when desires come your way
Are they joyous and purposeful and blessing your day
Choose wisely, my friend, befitting time and place
Yet allow thy child its share of fun-filled grace

For together in living harmony
Will you journey into the land of the free
And consummate the secret gift
Within the word Divinity

Willing To Will

Oh will of my mind in human slumber sleeping
Nestle in the Great Will that has you in its keeping
Relax thy small fire into Heart's Vast Altar Flame
And hear the Mother's gentle voice calling your name

Each thought, each person, each life sequence blending
Has reason and import beyond your wending
And as you give all respect that their wills may also be
Your humility and allowance opens doors to Eternity

Where the wind blows not and the flame doesn't burn
And the love of life you need not earn
For once Inside you'll join the Mother's Living Grace
And walk with Love's Spirit to fashion angelic lace

So that all on earth may become serene and free
Attuned to Higher Will for a united humanity

We Inherited Free Will

We inherited free will
To follow our desires until they become still
To learn from Love in our own chosen time
Sacrificing nothing to reach the sublime
Realizing that all within life's dreaming
Is divinely ordained, free of stress and scheming

Flames

Flames gone wild are called fire
Fire within mind kindles desire

When the flames upon mind's mountain top
     relax and become single
Then within heart's altar
     they can harmoniously mingle

With the serene energies of Soul
To warm God's Ultimate Goal:

True Love that's constant, open, and free
Evolving and expanding throughout eternity

Altaring The Flame

When the flames of latent desires
Scatter mind's outer fires
Relax all force and resistance
And in evenness witness
     their lively dance

Then merge each separate shaft of fire
Into one great candle's flaming spire
That floats lightly atop your brain
While singing a peaceful refrain

Then that which needed to be transmuted
Will be ordained and divinely recruited
To play its singular voice in harmony
Within God's universal symphony

I Ride A Broad Ocean

I ride a broad ocean on the crests of the waves
Feeling life through emotions that my moon displays

Without my desires how would life be
As quiet as a cork adrift on the sea

Or would there be a quality so refined
That it would elude my senses and everyday mind

And fill my chest with a spirit blessed
Of essential truths from Love's joyous nest

For who are we truly, just particles in a play
Dependent on overt movement within life's array

Or are we consciousness alive and unending
With a signature of attunements blending

If individuality be so ephemeral and amorphous unto my core
I pray to dream but of goodness that Love be my door

And all the rest of my sensory display
Either fall away
Or be redefined through a deeper knowing
That confirms to an Ideal that's ever growing

Into the Immaculate Expression of a Perfect Day

Chapter 6

Balance

Maintaining Integrity

I am like a temple that would touch a star
And if true to myself, I can reach quite far

Although you see but a piece of me,
        there's more for you to know
For my capacity lies deep within
        veiled from the outer show

Yet while connected to the wonders of life about
I learn to know myself inside and out

For only then can I maintain a balance perfect and rare
And walk anywhere without a care

Balance The Oneness With The Allness

Tell me, my child, what you want to be
And I shall tell you what you shall see

It all mirrors back—on the world's periphery—
Though the Gate of Truth is opened in solitary

Balance the Oneness with the Allness

Balance Thy Center

Balance thy center in crystal imagery

That when downward flows the Light
The Greater Ocean shall be made bright

And Heart shall be at peace
Even surface ripples to cease

Then clear will be thy picture through the earth
And in gentle potency will It gain Its new birth

Where Heaven at last will reign supreme
And Earth, thy Mother, will be its Queen

Allow Your Destiny

Given time and trust in God's Divine Plan
All events will be balanced by God's Mirrored Hand

That the Central Flow pro-Seed directly
Though to human eyes circumspectly

Thus exact Patience, Love, and a Smile
As you journey your destined mile

Simplicity

White horse, dark horse
              good and bad
Mind's gyrations
              make me sad
When all we need is but a simple key
To solve Life's Greatest Mystery . . . .

It's the ego imagining itself alone to be
That causes the Oneness of life to flee
Initiating mental patterns of Duality
Reflecting in the Cosmic Sea

Simplicity sees beyond creation's veil
Sight that glamour or credit would curtail
This doesn't mean responsibility should stand aside
But while within matter, in the Core one must abide

Then all things will be performed in wisdom's clarity
And the pressure of timing will become a rarity

It's only the Middle Path of the Central Tree
That allows one to be free within frequency
So whether at your job or in meditation's ecstasy
The Master's Sacred Key is Love's Truth & Simplicity

Breathing For Balance

When problems arise
I close my eyes
      and turn to my act of breathing:

In to the sky
      and the Father on High

Out to the earth
      and the Mother giving it berth

Forgetting self will in between
      ever eager to rule the scene.

In and up to the Father
Out and open to the Mother

In to the Father
Out to the Mother

Aligning my will to Their Flow
Centering it before letting go

And as Their Good issues therefrom
I give thanks when each problem is done

In a manner befitting a child of God
Honoring heaven and the Mother's green sod

Praise Duality

Praise duality and the teaching it gives
Guiding the free will in all that lives

Sentinels of energy and time forbearing
Imposing balance to all who are caring

To walk through to Oneness without restraint
Aligned in love's freedom without a taint

Of judgment, sorrow, or desires clinging
But with the joy and trust that all shall be bringing

To heaven's portals when they learn the true value of things
And merge with their God-Self to become masters of kings

Duality's Pendulum

Duality's pendulum is a living thing
That doesn't always swing
                              on a horizontal plane

But can reach many levels of time and space
And through mans participation can create
                              new conscious terrains

Where patterns of simple but evolving truth
Can easily be brought to the fore
And altar the life that accepts spirit's lure
And walks through its spiraling door

Chapter 7

Release

Invest thyself in the Spirit of Man, for therein lies the Holy Grail.
Release thyself unto the Whole. Thou needest not protect it.

Father Of The Wind

Like the waterfall or babbling brook
Father Wind circles round Mother Earth
Laughing over creation's boulders
Caressing Her and cleansing Her breath

Oh Father of the Wind, how little we know of your power
Invigorating earth's forms or making them cower

Your gentle breezes, your might and girth
Are but surface shows of your inherent worth

For you freshen the air, the breath of life
Your penetrate it, shape it, and free it from strife

Caused by contamination gained along the way
That would hide the beauty of creation's display

Often we turn our backs in your direction
For we know not of your true election

To clean and clear the dust from our mind
That the essentials may come forth to refine

Our perception of the pristine glory within all things
And the wondrous perfection in all that life brings

Muscle Power

The moon guides waves in and out
First this way, then that
But I want the tide to ever be full
To come to <u>me</u> where I'm at!

Should I use mind's muscle power
To alter its course
Or allow myself to dive deeper
And let go of force

      As I enter the Ocean of Being

        *   *   *

When I feel a tightness at the top of my head
Like muscles constricting to hold off a thought
I breathe through them with peace, light and love
And find that their stress becomes as naught

For I know this world is within God's Grace
And so I take His Loving Hand
And as I do, I free my Spirit
Once caught in my muscles' command

Releasing The Hold

May I relax in mind with my inner space wide open
And allow each loved one to cross heaven's Golden Ocean

Into The New and Beautiful, when their time has come
There to freely explore the Wholeness of One

Oh the subtlety of our holding onto things most dear
When in our letting go keeps their love ever near

Why do we have this subliminal fear of the Unknown
When we know that God is Love and Goodness full blown

Could it be that we have more faith in possessions' tight ruling
Than in Love's universal law of resonance spooling

If we could but cease the constrictive resistance of our mind
And open it in Love and Wonder for our kind

We'd help each person to release to their own peace and serenity
And find inner assurance of their unbroken integrity

And we too would know
        As we allow and let go
                That our union with them in heart's open space
                Will last beyond time and the confines of place

Freeing Outdated Judgment

Not far beyond the human sea
Is a realm that's open and free
Where neither criticism nor adversity reigns
And love and cooperation sustains

Gentle outpourings from this region of Light
Abound in soul's center giving us Sight
Glimpses of heavenly rays in our earthly realm
Encouraging us to let our soul take our helm
Whereby we can learn to exchange our limited "I love you"
For the greater agape that's timeless and true

But how do we do this without using mind's control?
An inner change of perception must be our goal

Instead of seeing the outer man reflecting
Look beneath to souls' purposes connecting
For their personalities have entered our experiential universe
Their divinely charted expressions to cultivate and nurse
Taking on the challenges that are most fitting
To beautify the living fabric that are knitting
So we may understand the results of actions past
Through the pain-pleasure matrix in which they were cast

For a hard life with many obstacles overcome
Will produce deeper understandings won
Than an easy life wherein few challenges are in play
To refine an entity within life's array

So with this knowledge of choice, born behind the scene
How can we judge one another within our earthly dream
As the class distinctions and body types that we see
Aren't valid criteria for discrimination in our outer sea

So in freedom let us take our stand
Honoring each and all as they live their plan
Bearing only their inalienable right
To walk with their soul in life, love, and light

Manifestation

Considered by some as an illusion
And by others a worldly effusion
Manifestation
Is truly the result of a contagion
Between variables that had gone before
And their resonance at matter's door

Thus for me manifestation is a trail's end
Of mind with matter and how they blend
For knowing that each end reflects it's beginning's need
By returning to the trailhead we find causation's seed

For it's not what we think we see
But the reality that caused it to be
That's most important to know
In order to enhance our life's flow

So as our illusions persist
May we not resist
Their overt display
And uncover the truth they convey

Obey Me!

Obey Me
And you can be free
Don't you see
All have a right to be . . . .

But until you relinquish your rules and commands
You will be subject to each other's demands
For each human ego tries to hold sway
Over its environment and finite array

Only when you renounce your self-made way of seeing
Will the greater world reflect Its true being
Then you can act with integrity to meet all demands
For in love and in freedom, you'll be holding God's Hands

Integrating The Reflections

Sometimes—

I find myself squinting as I look out at the world
As if for protection from things being unfurled
Yet in another space I know as well as I know my own name
That when integrated within, my outer world will be the same

So as with my meditations, unlimited and supreme
I open myself to all that I glean
And greet God and Self in our manifest scene
With the freedom and gratefulness within our love's dream

Just Because A Loved One Is Dead

Just because a loved one is dead
Doesn't mean your regrets can't be put to bed

For in an alternate way of emotional seeing
You can release your memories into positive being

Simply pray to your Self to purify the traits that you'd delete
And watch It call up real or symbolic scenarios for you to meet

Then using the newly learned understandings at your command
Open your heart and gentle your reaction to the situation at hand

Thereby freeing your partner(s) through newly created states
As you free yourselves' spectrum to regret-free slates

For in the higher spaces, time leavens not the problem's batter
And creating in dreams is akin to creating in matter

So carry no longer a sack of pain on your shoulders
But open it and discover its contents aren't boulders

And as you confront the fear-filled traits you held in your early life
You'll learn that freedom, love & harmony evaporates earthly strife

If I Should Need To Leave You

If I should need to leave you, pretend that I died
Think not the less of me for experiencing a circle wide

For when I return to Center, after all's said and done
I shall be more complete as I enter the Holy One

You now have a chance to strive toward Unconditional Love
To sweep back your outer layers and fly free like a dove

Removing the pangs of jealousy and self hurt
To gain the self-mastery your soul longs to exert

So come, my fair lady, think not of yourself
Allow God's Will freely, putting all else on the shelf

For if I had died wholly, how would you feel
You'd remember the good times that no one can steal

Yes, you'd feel lonely and some self pity too
But your wondrous faith would see you through

So now as a small part of me leaves, know you're well loved
Find your spirit within, and merge with your angels above

Overriding Guilt

At the root of desire is need
At the root of need is lack of true connection with the God within you
At the root of lack of true connection with your God is lack of self worth
At the root of lack of self worth is self-judgment and guilt
. . . . and guilt calls forth limitation
              and the voluntary entrapment of yourself
                    and your soul and the God within you.

So do you accept the guilt of your human mind's perceptions
And remain in the courtroom of your haunting imperfections
Or do you allow your soul to commune with you
Stepping out of this vortex to end your self's curfew

You are an out-breath of the God within and about you—
Now, allow Him to breathe you in.

Releasing Shame

When the cycle of shame is through
Let it release and dissolve in the blue
For harmonious attunement is the key
To a life that's joyous and free

For what's the good of a mindset of learning
That holds you down in your former mistakes
And thus forsakes
              The Christ Child inside
With whom you should consciously reside

So let the harsh disciplinarian fly
And become one with On High
Where Grace is a Word
That can be heard
When you're ready to herald a new beginning

Release Into Peace

Release your mind to Will's <u>freeing</u> refrain
To clean and clear your window's pain

You've had your turn
With less-ons urned

So react not to another's way
As they create their own play

Thinking not about self-connected coutours
But allowing instead all pre-scribed futures

For God can direct Life's Great Symphony
Far better than either you or me

Then your new world
Can be unfurled

And though seemingly more restricted
It's more inclusive and less conflicted

Giving your heart a new berth in open peace
For love through freedom to silently increase

Remember:
> *Silence is the Golden Key*
> *To Life, Love, and Mastery*

Chapter 8

Fear

Inclusive Consciousness

The speed of light heralds a fabric
Woven with threads of love . . . .

It cradles our realm of physicality
Within our three dimensional reality

Allowing mind to experience the patterns we would whirl
As our creative ideas we unfurl

But Consciousness carries not this restriction of light
And can sail beyond both black and white

Through a window so small and rare
That some say it's not really there

But which exists without boundaries—inclusive of all—
Of heights and breadths unfettered by our fall

So how do we get to this Holy Place
Remember Love, Gratitude, and Trust to embrace

For as you peel away layers of your outer self
To evaporate them from a heaven-sent shelf

They will release the energies they were holding
That no longer fit the personalities you are molding

And give you the opportunity
        To walk through them with impunity
                To a place of deep tranquility

So stay confident in the Process and be not afraid
For it leads to an Integrity where expanded truths are arrayed

Teaching you to walk through fear—an imaginary ploy of reflection
To that Freedom most dear and All Encompassing Perfection

Dealing With Worry

Don't let your mind scurry
When accosted by worry
For it's simply a residual fear
That by habit you've held near
For all fears of the unknown
Dissipate when faced full blown

Think of yourself as standing before a closed door
Behind which is a godsend that you have in store

You're ready for it or it wouldn't be there
So open yourself and stand without care

Then be patient, my friend, for your time to wax
Bringing on those frequencies that will help you max

Buried potentials yearning to be free
Helping to align you with your destiny

For the pattern of all life is growth and expansion
A chance toward greater good through divine ascension

Ascension neither linear nor channeled in the "up" direction
But spherical in nature towards an encompassing perfection

Wherein you purify with love and total acceptance
The lesser facets of self on your circumference

That they can be transmuted into sublime invisibility
To allow your world to be regaled in soul's sweet clarity

And as its spiritual wave issues further outward from your core
You might then find yourself before another waiting door

Flowing

Inspiration graces the heart and mind
As a gentle sun graces the waking earth
Freely, effortlessly, flowing imperceptibly
To enlighten and nurture seeds of worth

It delights in its quiet invisibility
Uncaptured by ego or the human condition
And simply flows downward, outward and through
Its pattern to ensue throughout manifestation

Resonance Is The Key

It's your resonance within creation's expanse
That invites you to your Cosmic dance

Nothing can be withheld
If, with it, you naturally meld

So relax all fears of being left out
For Love and Unity are what Life's about

Wasting Worry

Is my mind worried about me?
What a waste of energy!

Whether it goes up, down, or around
I am ever bound
To do what's right for me
The world, and humanity

For that was my pledge
'Ere I stepped over the ledge
Into incarnation's abyss
Receiving Love's Forgetful Kiss

So why should my mind be worried about me?
Because it used control to think itself free
Of the challenges associated with life on earth
And mistakes it might make causing pain and rebirth

Yet no matter how high it goes, it knows
That it's still attached to creation's shows
And to a facet of time to be wed
Until it consents to be put to bed

There to yield to heart's unifying grace
Exchanging its ambitions and upward chase
For the purposeful goals initially charted to be
Under the direction of divinity

Halloween

Halloween, where ghosts and goblins and witches abound
An outer show of man's fears manifestly gowned

But behind the masks that seem so real
Are eyes that twinkle when fear's revealed

For masks are but bait to bring out what's hidden
In one who's seeing that which he's bidden

'Cause after viewing one's shadow in a Halloween play
Comes the purification and awakening for All Saint's Day

———

A blessing it is to be approached by things
That tense your mind and tether your wings

For no matter where you are or what you do
Your charged emotions will reflect for you

Until you face & de-fuse them and send them on their way
Then fill their space with a more loving array

So remember that Halloween is hallowed cause it weans you from fear
That your being can be filled with what you hold dear

Welcome Problems

Very few new problems will come your way
On this or any other of your created days

For their seeds cycle short-comings in various settings
To teach lessons of self mastery not worth forgetting

So welcome all problems that come to your door
Gentle your reactions; find the solutions they store

To perfect your world and event-ually overcome
The younger parts of yourself, then merge with The One

Nothing Is Evil

Nothing is evil
       Nothing is dark
It's merely farther away
       From its counterpart

So judge ye not
       but unite us three
In a deeper, fuller
       and richer Me

Chapter 9

Allowing in Freedom

Where Freedom And Unity Merge
There doth emerge
The Sacred Flower
The Living dower
Of Soul Essence.

Become thou its fragrance

Love's Sacred Dance

As the blades of springtime grasses sway in a light rippling breeze
And the dancing flames of etheric fire around them
$\qquad\qquad\qquad$ radiate their Joy for life and growth

So may we participate in Love's Sacred Dance of Freedom
Where, without need of hands or eyes, only the relinquishment of self

Can our hearts sway within the inherent rhythm of becoming
As the meadow, the grass, and the tiny golden flames

Within the Great Oneness that IS.

Allow God To Happen

Your phases of life and life are like one, two, three
As prescribed by your own divinity

First comes the discovery and childhood play
Then life and living to seize the day

And finally, you're moving in evening's flow
Toward the fulfillment of all you know

By just allowing God to happen

Allow

Just because you're floating on the great Cosmic Sea
Don't forget to allow other worlds to be

For through their variations in density and aim
Comes the propensity for growth without shame

The quiet way, the simple journey
The love-lit path of God's returning

Allow all in space
To choose their pace

And heavenward you'll walk in serene understanding
Within a perfect statement of Cosmic Blending

Transparent To God

I walk a path through field and stream
Open to sun and shade within my dream
I see each person along the way
With smiling heart and joy at play

Soon after I'm working in the business world
Am I different with my analytic mind unfurled
Are those I encounter not just the same
As those ones in the fields from which I came

But the atmosphere seems crisper and sharper too
Than in my Mother's nature with her mantle of blue
Could this change affect my innermost being
Or be a conditioned way of outer seeing

Only knowing each person's God given soul
But not its personality, truths, or goal
How can I help enrichen its ongoing lives
Except to banish my opinions about its outer guise

And become completely open, transparent to God
That my fellow "me" can evolve free from the sod
And walk through each charted challenge, each self impelled urgency
To the fulfillment of his dreams within God's loving transparency

My Best Way

Open your mind
So that you can float
In the Breath of God
And become The Word of God.

When I think my way's the best,
Compare myself to another,
Or judge a situation,
My human mind picks up packages
That I must carry and give my attention to
To keep them alive.

And my outer ego grows like a balloon,
Expanding each time I reinforce these convict-ions,
Until I scarcely see beyond their confines

But as my burdens of ego expand
I feel my brain constricting
And I call it stress—
Until one day, I get tired of feeling it
And seek to open a window to relieve it.
Then as I let go of these comparisons
I begin to see eye to eye within the greater picture

And letting go of my self, I feel an Indescribable Space
Total Freedom—Selflessness—For a Magic Moment
As I go through the Eye of The Needle
As Air Ethereal

Possession

My hand is held flat and open to the sky
For the love that it holds comes from on High

Love that sits lightly, smiling, and at ease
Caressed by nature's warm summer breeze

I need not protect it for it's its own being
Aware of expanses beyond my finite seeing

Of the Wholeness that IS and what caused it to be:
God's Unlimited Perfection and The Mother's Nurturing Sea

So curl my fingers o'er my palm shall I not
For freedom within true Love is what I want

And when I awaken from the earthly dream that I'm in
This Love will encompass both my without and within

—:—

My hand is held flat and open to the sky
For the love it holds **freely** comes from on High

Mind Sets

With joy and expectation as to what the day will bring
And without prepared plans stretching desire's strings—

My child looks on with interest and wonder
And without a mind-set to be put asunder.

But do I see someone really doing something wrong
Or was that impression a warped judgment of the throng

That was set in place to improve conditions of the past
Which now can be released and discarded at last?

Does my child weigh his world by the standards he knows
Or by the beauty, potential, and lovingness it shows—

Beauty that may not appear within a single picture frame neatly
But will be magnificently clear when the film's shown completely

Prayer

Oh may my relationships be as free as a youth's in early spring
Marveling at nature and birds on the wing

May I embrace each breath of beauty directly by my beingness
Without thought of mind or surface seemingness

And may it not be held as particularly mine
But remain inviolate as an aspect of the Sublime

For as we leave all outer things free
Do we join more completely with the Inner Sea

Where we are truly One
        Smiling within The Inner Sun

Circles Within Circles

Circles within circles;
        spheres within spheres
What makes them distinguishable?
        Judgment, resistance, and fear

Yet within soul's circle,
        beyond light and dark
Is the Truth of ones being,
        without blemish or mark

It's here Heart sees truly,
        with total Love connecting
Bypassing created densities
        and mental mirrors reflecting.

Only when you approach this region
        of your consecrated core
Can you see the truth of others
        who knock at your door

Facing self-made challenges
        in each ring of separation
Caused by choices made
        and their resulting manifestation

And though those others are doing
        things you may dislike
If you remain in center,
        you'll help mitigate their blight

By using Love's energy
        when it's unconditionally needed
That through It's resonance
        disharmony can be weeded

So that one more ring
        of challenge and fear
Can dissolve in the charity
        of a heart ever near

The Quilting Party

Memories of situations and scenes that were seen
Some traits to remember and some to wean

Make up our colorful subconscious quilt
That over lifetimes we have unknowingly built

Each pattern is linked to our Self Divine
By a silver thread of Integral Mind

That relays information from our creative sea
To the Inner Template we're ordained to be

Then back from the Template the chosen thread's weaved
Carrying wisdom to follow that was Divinely conceived

An ordered exchange
Cosmically arranged

What are the guidelines that will lighten our quilt?
Love, Peace, and Freedom devoid of judgment and guilt

Treasures of Pure Essences
Freed by the acceptance of differences

Differences magnificent within multifaceted being
To the awakened Eyes of Universal Seeing

Positive Reactions

If you believe that God wants for you your ultimate best
Then no matter what greets you, you can always feel blest

And even if a challenge is given you in an inharmonious way
Your presenter might have been chosen in order that you portray

Specific attitudes and reactions which are latent in you
That need to surface and be cleansed through and through

The trick is in knowing the full power of God
To direct all of His children to raise their sod

Therefore, don't focus on the outer nor give it blame
But look to your reactions with clarity and not with shame

For we're all in the same divine school
Trying to live the Golden Rule

Wherein we're sometimes the teacher and sometimes the student
But whatever our role, we learn to be prudent

And remember that the outer scenario is not the important thing
But our loving reaction to each lesson is what makes our soul sing

Prayer:

May each less-on
   Remove all thoughts that do not aid
      That we may stand before our Creator
         With mind and heart unafraid

Divine Order

Divine Order fashions a heavenly lace
Woven by Love and patterned by Grace

The Bride of Spirit dawns this veil
That her soul's voice she might regale

Exchanging
        Personal will for gracious allowing
        Mental control for another's flowering
        Egoic stress for a world set free
        And self-made fate for Divine Destiny

Heart On

Heart on
        Hands off
                Mind open
                        One IS

Destiny

What God wants for me
Is what I Am and what i will be
Thus am i open to my destiny
In perfect trust and harmony

Grace

Resistance is a subtle thing
That stresses the mind and pins the wing
But Grace is full, limitless, complete
To enter its realm, true openness one must greet

Try to picture the facets of your personality
As myriads of stars without finality
Each a creative, distinctive part of you
Layers of expression through and through

Would you suppress one over the other
Youths seeking notice—your sister or your brother
"But I seek God and Christ's Spirit alone
I would place my soul near His Sacred Throne"

But thou art ever there within His Loving Grace
When each and all you would embrace
Allowing your Center the freedom to Be
Within the Magnificence of the Great Cosmic Sea

Lesson

Love thy many selves and one another
In thy inner world as well as thy outer
For unless you do
How can wholeness ensue
Whereby the All can become as One
Immaculate and Omniscient within The Son

Untethered Within The Beam

Through the night that I have made
I walk without fear, my mind unafraid

For I know that treasure of the eternal goal
Is the freedom of Heart joined with Cosmic Soul

No grasping after desires in the temporal scene
No judgments or opinions, just a God-centered beam

That shines unconditionally on both evil and good
Timeless in Love with Life's Quest understood

Untethered, my patient wings now fly
Into the brightness of a clear open sky

Chapter 10

Love

Unconditional Beingness

As you give unto the least of them,
                     so you also give unto Me

For unconditional Love is the Treasure
                     of God's Golden Sea.

Pure Love

Love that is tied to self
          is self love.

Love that is tied to an object
          is objective love.

Love that is tied to a subject
          is subjective love.

Be thee Pure Love—Whole and Free
Unconditional—as Love is meant to be

Heart's Alchemy

Within Air, Earth, Water, & Fire

Earth:

    Find out who you are
    Within our remnant of a star

Water:

    Let your emotions be even
    So as to bless all that is given

Air:

    Keep your thoughts pure and clear
    When seeking a Truth that's dear

Fire:

    When passions arise, altar their flame
    So that your will and God's will be the same

    Then when you amalgamate all four
    You can go through Life's Golden Door
    And with your soul personality be one
    Within the dimension of your inner sun

Love Penetrates All Veils

Just because you believe a loved one is dead
Doesn't mean you can't put your regrets to bed

For in an alternate way of emotional seeing
You can change your memories into positive being

Simply pray to your Self to purify the traits you'd delete
And watch it call up symbolic scenarios for you to meet

Then using the preprogrammed techniques at your command
React with heaven when each situation comes to hand

Thereby lifting your partner through your newly created states
As you release your mental sorrows and regret-filled slates

For in the higher spaces, time leavens not a problem's batter
And creating in dreams is akin to creating in matter

So carry no longer a sack of pain on your shoulders
But open it and discover its contents aren't boulders

Love, Human & Divine

Thank you for letting me love you . . . .

For touching my heart in its human space
And giving me a window to the divine embrace

For letting me see beyond the surface of things
Into the depth invisible that true love brings

For helping me ride through the changes of life
Knowing of a constant that's free of strife

That's ever-present within our hearts' divine space
And unconditional through God's Living Grace

Thank you for letting me love you . . . .

Because Of You

Though my life has ups and downs
They are gentler, because of you

Though my work is not profound
It's fulfilling, because of you

I know the heights, because of you
And know of God and rapture too

And my depths are warm
And fear's been shorn
And miracles exist
And love persists
And most of this
        Is
Because of you

Doorway To Love

Everyone has their special doorway to Love
A friend, a teacher, or someone above

That way-shower who leads you to life's total oneness
Through giving and receiving in absolute fullness

Where nothing is lacking and nothing is received
Beyond the parameters of the Great Will conceived

But on your journey to the Unfathomable Whole
Even the doorway must be walked through to reach Love's Goal

And its framework be well blest then allowed to go free
So it too can soar in heart's fullness to its ideal unity

Because the Love that each shares isn't limited by emotions or mind
As it is singular, all inclusive, and beyond a two-fold (di)vine

For not as a created thing, It IS and will always persist
As God's true living nature and His paramount bequest

Love Unsurpassed

I've never before experienced such an intensity
As that of my soul's love and its propensity
To merge with its true angelic mate
Within Heart's infinite Golden Gate

Like a loosed arrow, this swiftly moving feeling
Almost absorbed my self in its passion congealing
But Higher Will imbued with True Love's Freedom
Altared it's course and perfected its season

And gave my beloved to the Great All in all
To the Oneness we shared before our linked fall
So that now my beloved is in all of me
As I too belong to the Great Cosmic Sea

The Heart Of Lovingness

The Heart of Lovingness includes one and all
None singled out even after the fall

To consciously return to the Core of Love
Is to pledge your heart to the below and above

Thus replacing mans outgrown perceptions
With God's Unlimited Conceptions

Then one discovers that the laws of life can be understood
As but Love's offering toward the growth of The Good

Until once again Love and Truth in Oneness reign
And God's Wholeness is consciously regained

Devotion

As one gets closer to The One
            any one can become every one
                        and every one can become any one

Then truly:

> *That which ye do unto the least of them*
> *do ye also unto Me . . . .*

Thus it be wise to prepare your heart and mind
To serve the Essence of the Christ, the Mary, and the Divine

            with every breath you breathe
                        every thought you think,
                                    every act you perform

And, in Truth, that Essence of your devotion
Shall permeate humanity's subconscious ocean

Endless Renewing Through Love

Beyond the zone of fiery passion
Beyond all honors and accolades
Resides the band of Gentleness
And Wisdom unafraid

Heart's true aura of Lovingness
Enriching one and all
Enfolding earth in tenderness
And adjusting each karmic call

Knowing Beings all uniting
With Love's high purpose clear
Dissolving ambition's willful lust
And echoing God's Word near

We may call this mighty band
The working of God's Grace
But 'tis a field of The Pure and Sublime
As they their Journey embrace

For everything that IS and is ever to be
Is a spectrum of living motion
Patterned by will and frequency
Wandering in the Mother's Great Ocean

With particles releasing to ambient fields
And fields embracing their seeds
With Masters as Living Archetypes
And Spirit to meet greater needs

Yet in this fabric of living creation
Spiraling round One Central Core
Balance is maintained at every station
For a God so in Love He opened His Door

To one more layer of Self Sacrifice to Being
For the magnification of Omniscient Sea-ing

And God the One and GOD the All evermore are and shall be
United in Source through the Mother's Heart seeding Eternity

The Call To Love

The call for help is a beneficent thing
It flies through the air on angels' wing
Not always clarion, beautiful, or bright
But intended for those aspiring to heights

For as we are inwardly together, wholly and inseparably one
The same feelings are resident in us all 'til our divine work is done
And while we are helping to relieve the heartache of another
We are ridding from ourselves that pain we put asunder

So receive each call gladly when it resonates your being
And soon you'll become free of self-centered seeing
And be able to walk on mother earth's hallowed ground
With an open heart and divine consciousness to resound

Finally, remember when a cloud descends on you
That it might not be coming just out of the blue
But as a gift to make it very clear
That GOD's ever present and all are most dear

Wholeistic Evolvement

Air allows itself to be breathed.
Water allows itself to be drunk.
Plants allow themselves to be eaten.
Flowers allow themselves to be picked.

Each gives of itself unconditionally
that by their selfless acts of love,
all consciousness is raised.

Man, nurtured by loving Grace,
has the ability to enhance every aspect of life
when he learns to live
                    The First Commandment

Aspirations tossed into the blue
Will uplift a few
But a heart opened to the ocean of love
Heals a multitude through the Golden Dove

Chapter 11

Oneness

Convergence

Life is a portrait in dynamics: we see; we move; we get
Or we stand still—quiet—within ourselves
And that which resonates with us comes to us

Duality's poles create the dynamics
But between them, there's a space which is neither of them
Nothing—yet each and all of them—in total convergence
Containing the Peace of Wholeness—Intransitive Being

When you find yourself within neither part nor pole
Neither giving nor receiving
Going nor getting
Doing nor thinking
When the Pathway you are traveling comes to meet you
You are Home

Steadying The Flame

He whom Ye would have me be
And he whom Ye would have me see
Are one.

For as I am one with Ye
And Ye art he and me
No longer need there be
Triplicity

Thus desire is tamed by the Rose and the Flame
That the three "bodies" below
May know
Perfect alignment
And fulfill their assignment:
Total Peace Shared
And Godliness Bared

Transcendence

We create the symbols in the darkness of night
That we see in the forthcoming day
Patterns of remembrance and ideas of light
Gathered in holographic display

And each symbol created breathes in conscious life
Through the light and love of its maker
Yet simultaneously reflects the transient views
Of its receiving partaker

Only Mind transcending mind can see beyond
The forms that it's caused to be
And in the depths of Its being, at Its root and Its core
Can It dissolve them in the Cosmic Sea

Once more with The Mother, The Unifier of all
And destination of divine purposes blending
To bathe in Her midst after a Great Cosmic Day
Fulfilled by Pure Love-Light unending

Integration

If all of time and space is berthed in Love and Oneness
And if thy goals lie at the end of a space of time
Would not thine Ultimate Goal be more quickly reached
By taking time down unto its smallest segment?

So allow thyself fulfillment, O Man—
It is but a Moment away.

Inherited Riches

When our perimeters are in perfect order
We can walk freely through life's corridors
Doing deeds that fulfill needs
Ennobling man according to divine plan

In this **hour**
Money is not the dower
But an energy transformation that disappears from sight
As do most manmade things in the presence of Light

Even concepts of desire, judgment, fear and trust
Evaporate and return to dust
That once again will be lifted
And sifted
And born anew
In God's Sacred Wholeness with an Insight that's True

Then the riches of loving Oneness will enter and bless
Transmitting the Power of Compassion's tenderness
Which christens and nurtures Creation's Living Tree
The Divine Inheritance belonging to you and me

Successful

When you can rejoice at another's success
As completely as if it were your own
It will be—

For on the higher planes
It matters not whose success infills you
Only that it does . . . .

Releasing

God bless the Release that sensitivity brings
When expanding out into the world
For it makes me remember my knowledge of Truth
That we are all one being unfurled

So with that Truth exposed and clear
I free my halves and holds
And willingly dive in the Mother's Sea
To reflect our Father's Gold

Ordained In Unity

Where should personality end and unity begin?
Was individuality ordained or an original sin?

Granted, nothing is static, all is changing
And amorphous spectrums are rearranging

Breathing and weaving in and out
Through macrocosm and microcosm they wield about

Such that nothing is so special to have exclusive rights
To a thought, an idea, or ecstatic delights

But given free will, we can see in different ways
And our interpretations create the life of our days

Until we get tired of creation's manifest
And want to retire into unity's nest

There to give back the personality we've made
As we return to our Source, fulfillment displayed

Centering The Night's Flight

It's easy to keep unkind words away
When we pray throughout the day
To do the best that we can do
And hold our center 'til night is through

To quiet the mind through thick and thin
And maintain Integrity within each day's din
Thereby unifying all circumstantial sides
So that order and harmony can more easily abide

For only when perspectives are understood and known
Without the clutter of emotion's tone
Can Higher quiet the issues and guide us to what's best
So that peace, joy, and love can permeate our nest

So on it goes as our purification takes place
Until one day we reach the end of our race
When time evaporates and space becomes a new land
As we amalgamate into God as the Wholeness of Man

Chapter 12

God and Prayer

God: Becoming The Template

God is Unconditional, Self-Fulfilling, and One
      Seeing the spectrum of all within
Giving of Himself, His Breath and His Being
      Knowing that all are irrevocably Him

How can we imitate a GOD such as this
      Within such an infinite frame
Living as we do in a finite world
      With our terribly limited brain

Through <u>Unconditional Love</u> comes the Fullness we seek
      Within the Freedom of Being
Where the very essence of Its Wholeness
      Embraces our world of seeing

But awareness of particulars we've diligently learned
      Through incarnations borne in time
So it's no easy challenge to free negative thoughts
      From our human analytical mind

To trust our heart and allow matters to flow
      In their destined, God-guided course
Setting aside self for evolvement's sake
      Without conditions or remorse

For a Template was seeded within our soul
      Ordaining us to function such as He
Expansively, Fruitfully, Wisely, and Lovingly
      As was His/Our Conception to Be

So on through lifetimes we persevere
      As particles in an infinite field
Until that day when our Macrocosmic Self
      Will seamlessly be revealed

Love's Prayer

An adaptation of The Lord's Prayer

Our Father who art in Heaven
Our Mother who art in Earth
Hallowed be Thy Names

Thy Kingdom come; Thy Will be done
Thy Compassion come; Thy Love be One
On Earth as it is in Heaven

We thank Thee this day for our daily bread
And for our deep trust and faith in Thee

Forgive us out trespasses
While teaching us to understand
Thy First Sacred and Holy Command

As we walk through the valleys of temptation
May we be ever conscious of Thy Presence
Delivering us from seeming evil

For in Thee is the Kingdom, and the Power,
The Love, and the Glory
Now and forevermore

Amen

In Reverence

Oh Sphere of Life and Sphere of Knowing
You are my consciousness ever growing
Transmuting each purification request into Light
To reveal my highest heights and darkest nights

Tenderly did you hide my youthful follies within your loving veil
Until through patient love they could be repatterned then regaled
Reaching beyond human desires and willful fate
Into Divine Destiny's unified template
There to expose Thy Mysteries to selfless eyes
Within the realm of our Oneness, the Joy of the Wise

A Prayer Of Gratitude

May I love as I have been loved
May I serve as I have been served
And may I be as open and accepting
        as the air I breathe
        the water I drink
        and the earth that cushions my feet

As the planets orbit near and far from their central sun
May I love each space that I find myself within and open fully to it
Knowing there is purpose and good in all expressions

As Life's Dance spirals onward . . . .

Prayer Is For Attunement

God is everywhere, all the time
Within every creation, ridiculous or sublime
And through Love and Grace and Laws proclaimed
He guides us to Truths purposely aimed

Love's Union is His Goal and Peace His Link
He's all pervading, yet manifests what we think
Giving us prayers for attunement, not to order Him about
For He knows everything already so we don't need to shout

For He's never absent, though at times we may be
So remember Him daily, His Oneness to see
And when it comes that you find Him inside
You'll know within others He doth also abide

Therefore speak to your brother as you'd speak to your God
No demands or conditions, with trust not a rod
And attunement will follow where Love and Joy abound
Riding on the Soul's Stream of God's Peace Profound

O Man of infinite potential
I bow to the God within You
And to your inalienable divinity
I trust I'll ever be true

My Father

My Father is a prince of peace
Filled with Grace that will never cease

And though we picture Him mantled in white
The Energy He wears is full-spectrum Light

To revere such a One is a noble thing to do
But to have Him in your heart bespeaks the wonder of you

For enshrined within this chamber of pristine love
Is His Word unspeakable per the angels above

This is His Gift to every Man
His Shrine of Beingness that few understand

That can never be diminished in eternity of time
As it is the Source and Wholeness of Life Sublime

Creating Yourself

If you could co-create yourself with the help of God
To live life again on earth's haloed sod
And consciously receive 10 sovereign wishes
To sew traits of character with masterful stitches
What would you ask for
As you open incarnation's door?

To give all I know freedom and a chance to grow
While offering only love and grace to evolving space

To be in the heart of lovingness and have a mind that's clear
To feel the fullness of music and the natural beauty that's here

To accept with gratitude those challenges that make me kindly & strong
And erase the residual habits that in heaven don't belong

To have parents, friends, and family who are free to follow Heart's Word
And for me an ability to know soul's guidance when heard

And finally, to maintain a will that's true within our Creator's Scheme
So that under His Auspices, all shall realize The Immaculate Dream

The God Of Our Gods

Be as a Star, a Sun of Pure Thought
Carrying Its Light into the Womb of the Night

And then while in Thy Mother's tender embrace
Walk as a Child, fully open to Grace

For in this way can Thy God Parents be more fully Lighted
And once again with *Their* "Unknowable" GOD be reunited

So that their GOD can make ITS Journey to our time-space dimension
To fathom our birthing within creation's ascension

With Greater Awareness
Within Absolute Wholeness

Simply Prayers

Dearest God, may I see Love through Your Eyes
Thy Essence within Thy many forms
The Light and Wisdom of Thy Wondrous Plan
And the Bliss and Joy of Truth and Beauty unfolding

God, please keep my heart ever open to Thee
Excluding none that all might be
Living and Loving Consciously

God, please keep my mind always centered in Thee
Throughout this portion of Eternity
That I may not plant in time or space
Any thought or feeling that would disgrace
Thy Perfect Plan

Release My Ignorance

O pride—O ego in your self appraised perfection
Are you willing to open yourself to undaunted circumspection?
Are you willing to go through the celestial gates
In order to perform loving service within My Estates?

I answer You in humility of spirit
As I would follow Thy Calling when I hear it

For my deepest plea is to rid my world of ignorance
And care for those I love without hindrance

So that they may be free to swim the Mother's Sea
With hearts in joy and minds in charity

That all regrets be things of past
Replaced by timeless values that last

O Dispeller of Illusions of Grandeur
Allow my world to reflect Truth through candor

Release my ego's resistance
And give me Thy divine assistance

Do for me whatever it will take
To dispel my ignorance for Thy Love's sake

Miscellaneous

Disease

Disease is not mysterious
        But ease that's simply been dis-ed
By thoughts, emotions, or unwise acts
        That your freewill allowed to be kissed

For unless you feed upon judgment or fear
        Instead of Love's fullness and ease
Neither germ nor seed from some unknown source
        Can foster you ill will or disease

Your world is a mirror showing all facets of you
By your reaction to it, your good can ensue
For assistance to all amalgamates higher being
While resistance is the veil that separates our seeming

Resistance can also be a disease-holding thing
As it precludes your toxins from taking wing
Bottling them up in a nice little cyst
So that their cycle for deliverance can often be missed

Then they'll lie hidden in your being
Until brought forth by an act of seeing
Something that resonates with them in your outside world
That allows them to manifest themselves unfurled

So instead of resisting that which you don't like "out there"
Allow your re-cysting to stop and toxins to leave your lair
Without hesitation and the fear of opening a can of worms
For, cushioned by love, they are but lessons by which to learn

Depression's Dowry

In the depths of deep depression
We can find life's true expression

For in that state of darkness delving
Only prime denominators can bypass shelving

As there the basic truths of life still prevail
And shine their light through illusion's veil

The seed that lifts its head to the sky
The flower that opens when morning is nigh
The heart that beats between tiny breasts
The self that awakens to love's tenderness

All remind us that life's an journey toward the Sun
From which we descended as Seeds of The One

So smooth out that depression with the kindness of the day
Until you can laugh at your learning within Life's Great Play

Pleiadian Teachings: Color Codes

Pink is the universal color of love
That opens our hearts to set free the dove
So use this color when you begin to attune
Thereby to bypass mind's reflecting moon

Then for spiritual healing, use life-giving **green**
To underscore your love and paint the scene

Thereafter comes beautiful sky **blue**
To cultivate trust that Higher ensue

Next are **golden** sprinkles showering from on High
Bringing Grace to the subject and all he stands by

Violet or purple eventually sheds its beam
Allowing transformation to make the scene

And finally comes **yellow**, illumination's prize
That ushers in the **white**, Christ's Light without guise

If you would attune with universal beings
Pursue their color tone way of seeing
And watch your challenges evaporate more easily
And your planetary work escalate more feasibly

An Invitation Home: Consolation

On the Ladder of Infinite Levels of Being
GOD has His Own Way of Absolute Seeing

For in His Heart of Love and Wisdom combined
Is Truth that's Knowing beyond Human Time

That Heart your beloved has touched and made their own
And It's extended to them an Invitation Home

To help The Father fulfill His Plans most dear
And The Mother to carry them in Compassion far and near

We treasure your beloved with our hearts open wide
And know there will always be a place within us for them to reside

As they work with the Light-filled Blessed Trinity
And embrace our spirits in God's Loving Unity

Support Yourself

The angelic beings from on high
View in us all the potential to fly
Even those whose acts do not quite fit
Into the template they originally knit

Nevertheless, Higher always offers its support
To the heartfelt projects we willingly court
Giving never-ending, unconditional love
That the fluttering wings of our inner dove—

May enliven our true soul quest
And propel our minds from the amnesiatic nest
To become a servant of one and all
In remembrance of Life before our fall

O pray thee well to remember that time
Before you drank your self-made wine
That split your golden bond of loving unity
Into particles of multiplicity

For now the hour is here to support each life-form you see
So that the all of you can be one again with a greater Living Tree
Tarrying not by a focus on the outer manifested rings
But bathing in the fullness that our inner Life-Stream sings

Support—Support—Support—
And none can thwart
The divine plans that wouldst manifest
Through your/His/our loving hands

A Dandylion In The Wind

I know a little of much but with whom can I share
So I smile at the sun and scatter my seeds in the air

I awoke in a cocoon small and warm but felt a yearning to arise, so I stretched myself upward until I found myself surrounded by green grass. It took a little while, but soon I was able to lift up my head and see blue skies above me, and a great yellow light in its midst—and there were golden rays that streamed from that light, bright rays that sang to me and warmed me and gave me life.

In the days that followed, I became aware of everything happening within me and around me. I loved hearing the sun and the earth singing together, the trees murmuring their deep voices with each other at their roots, and the stream dancing in delight at daybreak at the edge of the forest. And then, there were my friends in the green meadow all around me. So happy was I in my life that I wanted to share my joy in being; and when this desire filled myself, I noticed little flags, golden like the sun's rays growing outward from my heart.

I called these little flags "petals" and waved them gently at passersby, hoping they would listen to the story of my growth. But, nay, the bees were to busy to stop their work and the ants were too interested in what was about them on the earth to look up. The grasses sang sweetly, gentle songs, but they didn't know what it was like to have a flower grow from within them, so they just smiled—and I kept to myself.

Time passed. Everyday I greeted the sun, trying to be his beauteous reflection, and my heart grew bigger and bigger with my love for him. Then one morning, I noticed the tiniest little white flowers springing directly from my heart, each reaching skyward. And as they stretched themselves toward the sun's welcoming light, I grew contented and settled into myself. And though I still had a wealth of understanding and joy to share, I released it all into those little heart flowers and watched as each grew white feathers of truth and knowing. The last thing I can remember of them was that they looked like the lightest, softest, full moon that you could imagine. After that, I felt so blessed that I went deep within the roots of myself. I was not even aware when the first winds of autumn blew my moon children apart, scattering them as seeds around me.

I don't know for how long I slept, contented in my soul, but once again I awoke and sprang to life, and after pushing upward, when I looked around, I found others like myself already awake and reaching out new yellow petals in their joy of life—and the sun was smiling and singing a wondrous song of love to my nurturing mother, and all was right with my world.

Index

Page